Ethics is knowing the difference between what you have a right to do and what is right to do.

- Supreme Court Justice Potter Stewart

The consequence of winning is one of the most common desires of persons affiliated with sport. Athletes, coaches, and sport managers act in ways to achieve victory. If they are guided exclusively by their desires to win, moral reasoning most likely will not be a part of the process involved in winning.

- Robert C. Schneider

Ethics and Sports

20 True Stories with Moral Implications

Max Malikow

Ethics and Sports

ISBN 9781737264521

Dedications

To Rabbi, Dr. Earl A. Grollman: My mentor, counselor, and friend who departed in October. I miss you.

To Rocco Gonnella: A great all-around athlete and devoted follower of Jesus Christ.

To Pat Ryan: "My Captain" and a truly decent human being.

Preface

I've long wanted to write a sports book but academic demands, including teaching moral philosophy, prevented the book you are reading. Serendipitously it occurred to me to combine one interest (moral philosophy) with another (sports) into a collection of stories.

After reflecting on my favorite sports stories I noted that many of them have a moral component. The ease with which I found either an instance of moral excellence or discovered an ethical issue in each story reassured me that morality and sports are intertwined.

Max Malikow
Syracuse, New York
February 17, 2022

Introduction

These are not stories of record breaking performances in sports. Some are stories of individuals who displayed moral excellence and others about athletes whose behavior elicits a moral question. Interesting is some of these figures seem to have done something that oppose what others have done. Joe Louis was obedient to his country while Muhammed Ali defied it. Yet both men acted from conviction. A. Bartlett Giamatti eloquently condemned cheating while Denny McLain showed kindness by breaking the rules. Most people would agree with Giamatti intellectually yet emotionally appreciate what McLain did.

Such is the nature of ethics – the subcategory of philosophy that addresses the principles of right conduct. Often moral right and wrong cannot be reduced to a binary choice. As with many of life's issues, the right position is located in a shade of gray between black and white.

Table of Contents

STORIES OF MORAL EXCELLENCE

One way to characterize heroism is an action that expresses a virtue to an extraordinary degree. Although morality and heroism are not synonymous they are closely related, making each of these accounts a heroic story. Each of the stories in this section provides a demonstration of one or more of the following virtues: integrity, compassion, faithfulness, conviction, perseverance, commitment, justice, self-discipline, wisdom, resilience, and determination.

1. Joe Louis: The Debt

Joe Louis is a credit to his race, the human race.

-Jimmy Cannon

Integrity is the quality of being of sound moral principle. People with integrity are honest, sincere, and honorable. Fred Rogers ("Mister Rogers") addressed integrity when speaking at the Boston University commencement: "Always behave in such a way that you'll never be ashamed of the truth about yourself." (1992) Boxing legend Joe Louis never had to be ashamed of the truth about himself. He showed himself to be a man of integrity in his toughest fight, the one he had with the Internal Revenue Service.

After his last fight a concerned doctor carefully studied Joe Louis' swollen and lumpy face. "Joe, you can't fight for at least three months," said Dr. Vincent Nardiello as he shone his small flashlight into the fighter's eyes.

"Doc," Louis responded, "Do you mind if I don't fight any more at all?" (McRae, 2002, 1979)

On the morning of October 26, 1951 Jimmy Cannon described middle-aged, battle-worn Joe Louis:

> He is an honorable man of simple dignity who works at the dirtiest of all games with a crude nobility. As a pugilist this is a guy whose deportment matches his skills. Even now, at thirty-seven, slow and often clumsy, Louis is a reliable performer. The errors he makes are caused by a disobedient body. But his gameness is unimpaired and his intentions are pure. (Cannon, 1951)

Cannon's sentimentality for the man who was the heavyweight champion of the world for 11 years came from memories like the one in 1948 after the first Joe Wolcott fight. Although Louis won, "His face was swollen. He looked like a loser" writes Cannon. (1951) But before he could ask his first post-fight interview question, Louis remembered that Cannon had not been feeling well and asked him, "How's your cold?" (1951)

On October 26, 1951 Joe Louis stepped into the ring to face Rocky Marciano in a non-title fight. Louis had retired in 1949, leaving the title to be claimed first by Ezzard Charles and then Joe Wolcott. Marciano was a rising star who would eventually wrest the heavyweight championship from Wolcott. Well aware that his best days were behind him, Louis came out of retirement in 1950 intending to earn enough money to settle a $500,000 tax debt owed to the Internal Revenue Service.

Generosity, patriotism, reckless spending, and misplaced trust combined to erode the fortune he had accumulated over a 17 year career.

> When he earned over $371,000 in his first two years as a professional boxer, Louis immediately helped family and friends all over the country. For example, he voluntarily paid back to the government welfare payments his stepfather had received during the Great Depression. One month after the bombing of Pearl Harbor, the generous Louis gave his entire $65,200 fee (about $700,000 in today's money) from a fight to the Naval Relief Fund. Less than three months later, he gave his $45,882 purse from another fight (about $500,000 today) to the Army Relief Fund. Ever the Patriot, he halted his lucrative boxing career and enlisted as a private, earning only $21 a month. (McRae, 2002, p. 275)

Ironically, the total of Louis' donations to the war effort ($111,082) was nearly equal to his original tax debt ($117,000). Unfortunately, by the time the IRS made him aware of his debt the interest on it increased it to over a million dollars. In addition to the original debt he was being taxed on the money he was earning in his effort to pay off the debt. Reflecting on this Sisyphean task, he said "When you owe that kind of money you can't get out…it's like doing roadwork on a treadmill. The faster you run, the faster they move that treadmill against you." (McRae, p. 288).

It's unfortunate that of the innumerable photographs of Joe Louis the one most famous is from the Marciano fight and the least indicative of Louis' greatness. It shows him dazed and flat of his back, his body draped over the ring's bottom rope. Marciano felt so bad about the beating he gave his boyhood idol that Rocky cried and apologized to Louis after the fight. The ex-champion thanked the future champion for agreeing to the match and an opportunity for a payday. Louis earned $135,000 that night, most of which he turned over to the IRS.

Also regrettable is that the Marciano fight was not the "Brown Bomber's" final humiliation. Although it was his last boxing match, it was not the last time he entered the ring. Desperate for money, in 1956 he turned to professional wrestling. Balding and paunchy, Louis was as embarrassed by his aging body as by the pseudo-athletic farce in which he was participating. Before his quixotic effort to settle with the IRS was over he would further lower himself by appearing on television game shows. Even when he and his wife, Rose, managed to win $60,000 on the show "High Finance," his $30,000 share went to the IRS. As if to prove that humiliation knows no depth, the champion traveled with a circus as a make-believe lion tamer. Armed with a whip, he feigned mastery over a lion who, like Louis, had grown old and devitalized.

It has been said that members of the United States Congress would vote to exempt themselves from the law of gravity if they could. Yet

Congress showed no regard for Louis' wartime generosity when they voted to reject a bill proposed by Alfred Sieminski (Democrat, New Jersey) to forgive Louis' tax debt. Those who voted "no" on that proposal seem quite unlike the man of whom sportswriter Milton Gross wrote: "He was a symbol of integrity. He was a man of unimpeachable pride and steadfast principle." (p. 297)

Question

Was Louis' determination to pay the debt a demonstration of integrity or capitulation?

2.   Floyd Patterson: Giving Sonny a Chance

In the films the good guy always wins, but this is one bad guy who ain't going to lose.

- Charles "Sonny" Liston

The only thing Floyd Patterson and Sonny Liston had in common was boxing's heavyweight championship of the world. Patterson held the title from 1956 to 1959 and 1960 to 1962. (He lost the title to Ingemar Johansson in 1959 and regained it one year later in a legendary knockout that left Johansson unconscious for five minutes.) Liston held the title from 1962 to 1964 before losing it to Muhammed Ali (then Cassius Clay).

The soft-spoken Patterson was a gentleman, the glowering Liston was a thug. Patterson was an Olympic gold medalist, Liston had been arrested 19 times, including arrests for armed robbery and assaulting a police officer. Patterson was refined as a boxer by the renowned trainer Cus D'Amato, Liston learned boxing while in prison. Even their styles were different. Patterson was schooled in the evasive "peek-a-boo" defense to take advantage of his lightcning reflexes. Liston, although highly skilled, depended on a jab that could stop a man in his tracks and power punches that were "finishers." George Foreman, who sparred with Liston, said Sonny was the only man whose jab made him back up. Liston knocked out seven of Wayne Bethea's teeth with a single punch and another opponent, Nino Valdes, when dying from cancer, said it didn't hurt as much as being hit by Sonny Liston.

Patterson was small for a heavyweight, weighing less than 200 pounds, but hit with cnough power to compete with bigger fighters. Liston was a thick-muscled 215 pounds and looked 20 pounds heavier.

His extraordinary 84 inch arm reach was equal to that of a man seven feet tall while Patterson's was a more normal 71 inches. On merit, if a man ever deserved a title fight it was Liston. For two years he walked through the heavyweight division beating ranked fighters Patterson avoided. It wasn't a lack of courage on Patterson's part but D'Amato's management that accounted for the selection of opponents. D'Amato knew big, hard hitters like Mike DeJohn and Cleveland "Big Cat" Williams posed a threat to the champion and were sidestepped. (Liston fought both and knocked both out.) Liston's criminal past and well-known mob connections provided a convenient excuse for denying him a title shot. Moreover, the NAACP discouraged Patterson from fighting Liston, fearing Sonny would be a negative role model for Black youth. Even President Kennedy communicated to Patterson his preference that he not fight Liston.

Patterson carefully listened to President Kennedy but responded, "I'm sorry Mr. President, the title is not worth anything if the best fighters can't have a shot at it. And Liston deserves a shot." (Levy, 2008, p. 137) In an interview with sportscaster Howard Cosell, Patterson said, "if there is someone out there who can beat me in a fair fight, I'd rather he have the crown than I." (p. 125)

Eventually Patterson overruled D'Amato and agreed to a title defense against Liston. Patterson reasoned since Liston had a license to box he was eligible to fight for the title. On September 25, 1962 the champion entered the ring an 8:5 underdog against the challenger. Two minutes and six seconds after the opening bell Sonny Liston was the heavyweight champion of the world. Before the fight D'Amato had expressed his concern that his fighter lacked what Liston had: "Floyd lacks the killer instinct," D'Amato complained when it became impossible for him to shield Patterson from Liston's menacing shadow. "He's too tame, too nice to his opponents. I've been trying all the psychology I can think of to anger his blood up, but he just doesn't have the zest for viciousness." (McRae, 1999)

John L. Sullivan, the last bare-knuckle heavyweight champion, is reputed to have announced, "I can lick any man in the house" when entering a tavern. Another champion, Joe Louis, said he wouldn't feel like the champion until he defeated the man who had knocked him out the year before he won the title. Unlike Sullivan, Patterson never boasted he could "lick any man in the house." Like Louis he couldn't consider himself the true champion until he defeated the most dangerous man in the house.

Patterson feared Liston, as did every other man who fought him, including Muhammed Ali. But Patterson had the courage to get in the ring with him when he didn't have to. Franklin Roosevelt said, "Courage is not the absence of fear, but rather the assessment that something else is more important than fear." (2022) Floyd Patterson was a man of courage and integrity.

Postscript

In an attempt to regain the title Patterson fought Liston again a year later with the same result – a first round knockout.

Question

Do you agree with Patterson's decision or with those who didn't want Liston to be the champion?

3. Jack Twyman: His Brother's Keeper

If not me, then who? If not this, then what? If not now, then when?
- Attributed Variously

Theologian and philosopher David Elton Trueblood writes, "A man has at least made a start on discovering the meaning of human life when he plants shade trees under which he knows full well he will never sit." (1951, p. 58) Jack Twyman planted a tree that gave him no benefit but provided shade for Maurice Stokes.

In a word, Maurice Stokes was a terror. Expanded to two words, he was a rebounding terror. Playing for St. Francis, a small college in Pennsylvania, he averaged 25 points and 25 rebounds per game in the early 1950's. Selected in the first round of the 1955 NBA draft, he didn't seem to notice the difference between small college and professional basketball. Playing for the Rochester (later Cincinnati) Royals Stokes was the 1956 NBA Rookie of the Year and set an NBA rebounding record the following season, averaging 17 rebounds per game. Until the arrivals of Bill Russell and Wilt Chamberlain he was the greatest rebounder in NBA history.

And then, on March 12, 1958, his hall-of-fame career ended in tragedy. In the last game of his third season he took what appeared to be an ordinary fall. But it wasn't ordinary, it was catastrophic. Maurice struck his head on the hardwood floor and what started as a headache became seizures and culminated in irreversible quadriplegia. The diagnosis was post traumatic encephalopathy.

Although teammates on the Royals, Twyman and Stokes were not especially close. Still, Twyman had a sense of calling. In the New Testament one of the parables told by Jesus is the Parable of the Good Samaritan. (Luke 10:25-37) Jesus told it in response to the question, "Who is my neighbor?" The answer is whoever you encounter who's helpless and in need is your neighbor. This is not to say Jack was inspired by his Sunday school education. (Although he did graduate from Central Catholic High School in Pittsburgh, Pennsylvania.) Whatever his motivation the spirit of the Good Samaritan resided within him.

For the next 12 years Jack was Maurice's legal guardian and raised funds for his care. His effort included an annual charity basketball game featuring NBA players participating pro bono. (This was not your father's NBA.) Jack helped Stokes to obtain workers' compensation and taught him to communicate by blinking his eyes to denote individual letters. Later, when Stokes was able to type, his first message was: "Dear Jack, How can I ever thank you?" (Martin, 2012)

Maurice died in 1970 at the age of 36, long before "Black Lives Matter" became a national call to action. Jack Twyman, who died in 2012 at 78, was White. Maurice Stokes was Black. Jack got the BLM memo before it was written.

Postscript

How good a basketball player was Maurice Stokes? In September 2004 he was inducted posthumously into the Naismith Memorial Basketball Hall of Fame. His three year production was so impressive the selection committee projected he would have had a hall of fame career had he not been injured.

Question

What motivated Jack to take on the responsibility of providing for Maurice's care?

4. Muhammed Ali: Conscientious

How does it become a man to behave toward the American government today? I answer, that he cannot without disgrace be associated with it.
- Henry David Thoreau

Civil disobedience, a term identified with Henry David Thoreau, is the belief that individuals should not permit governments to overrule their consciences and they have a duty to refuse to cooperate with any government policy or action the individual deems immoral. The Rev. Dr. Martin Luther King, Jr. wrote of Thoreau's influence on him:

> During my student days I read Henry David Thoreau's essay On Civil Disobedience for the first time. Here, in this courageous New Englander's refusal to pay taxes and his choice of jail rather than support a war that would spread slavery's territory into Mexico, I made my first contact with the theory of nonviolent resistance. Fascinated by the idea of refusing to cooperate with an evil system, I was so moved that I reread the work several times. I became convinced that noncooperation with evil is as much a moral obligation as cooperation with good. (1998, p. 14)

In the spirit of Thoreau and King, Muhammed Ali refused induction into the United States Army in 1967. He claimed exemption from the military on religious grounds and opposition to American involvement in Vietnam:

> War is against the teachings of the Qu'ran. I'm not trying to dodge the draft. We are not supposed to take part in no wars unless declared by Allah or The Messenger (Elijah Muhammed,

the leader of Nation of Islam). We don't take part in Christian wars or wars of any unbelievers. (01/12/2021)

When he appeared for his scheduled induction into the United States Armed Forces he refused three times to step forward when his name was called. By refusing induction he was committing a felony punishable by five years in prison and a $10,000 fine. He was arrested and later that day the New York State Athletic Commission suspended his boxing license and stripped him of his title. He was unable to obtain a license in any state for the next three-and-a-half years. Deprived of his livelihood, he travelled the country making public appearances earning far less than he had as a fighter. Desperate for income, he appeared in a Broadway musical ("Buck White") that was cancelled after five days. His trainer, Angelo Dundee, summarized the price Ali paid for refusing to serve by saying, "One thing must be taken into account when talking about Ali: He was robbed of his best years, his prime years" (2012). A conservative estimate of how much Ali would have earned during those years is 3.5 million dollars. (Likely he would have fought twice a year and earned at least $500,000 for each fight.)

On June 28, 1971 the Supreme Court unanimously overturned Ali's conviction. The Court held that since the appeal board did not give a reason for denying his conscientious objector status it was impossible to determine if the board had erred. On this basis, Ali's conviction was reversed. During his exile from boxing he spoke at a college campus and explained his refusal to serve in the military:

> My enemy is the white people, not Viet Cong or Chinese or Japanese. You my opposer when I want freedom. You my opposer when I want justice. You my opposer when I want equality. You won't even stand up for me in America for my religious beliefs—and you want me to go somewhere and fight, but you won't even stand up for me here at home. (Metz, 2013)

William Rhoden, formerly a *New York Times* columnist and currently a writer-at-large for ESPN, writes admirably of Muhammed Ali:

> Ali's actions changed my standard of what constituted an athlete's greatness. Possessing a killer jump shot or the ability to stop on a dime was no longer enough. What were you doing for the liberation of your people? What were you doing to help your country live up to the covenant of its founding principles? (2013)

Boxing promoter Bob Arum did not support Ali's decision when he refused induction. However, in an interview 50 years later, he said,

> (W)hen I look back at his life, and I was blessed to call him a friend and spent a lot of time with him, it's hard for me to talk about his exploits in boxing because as great as they were they paled in comparison to the impact that he had on the world. He did what he thought was right. And it turned out he was right, and I was wrong. (Whitcomb, 2016).

Question

Is there an inconsistency between Ali's life as a professional fighter and his refusal to serve his country as a soldier?

5. Andea Jaeger and Shelly Pennefather: A Calling

God did not call me to be successful. He called me to be obedient.

- Mother Teresa

In 1981 sixteen-year-old Andrea Jaeger, the youngest player to be seeded at Wimbledon, was ranked second among women playing professional tennis. In 1987 Shelly Pennefather completed her stellar career as a college basketball player at Villanova University. A first team All American in 1987 and three time Big East Player of the Year (1985, 1986, and 1987), Pennefather was awarded the Wade Trophy in 1987, given to the outstanding women's collegiate basketball player. She remains Villanova's all-time leading scorer for both women and men with 2,408 points. Harry Perretta, her college coach, said of her,

> When I had Shelly Pennefather (in the mid-1980's), I used to try to dream up ways we could possibly lose. But about 24 minutes into a game, reality sets in and you realize there's no way you can lose. (Berlet, 1995).

Jaeger earned $1.4 million dollars in prize money over her five year career in addition to even more in endorsements. (Her career was cut short by a shoulder injury.) Pennefather played professional basketball in Japan for three seasons, eventually receiving a six figure salary offer. Both women had a calling. For Andrea it was the Silver Lining Foundation, a camp for children with cancer and other life-threatening illnesses. Located in Aspen, Colorado, it was largely financed by her tennis earnings. She later relocated the foundation to Florida, renaming it the Little Star Foundation. In 2006, at age 41, she became Sister Andrea, an Anglican Dominican nun. She left the sisterhood before taking her final vows when she realized she would not be able to spend enough time on her various philanthropic interests and fulfill the obligations required of her as a nun. This was similar to her previous realization that she could not devote herself to tennis and fulfill her desire to help others.

For Shelly it was a calling to the monastic life. In 1997, six years after entering a monastery in Virginia as a novice, she took her final vows as a nun. Now named Sister Rose Marie, she didn't have physical contact with her family until 2019 and will not see them again until 2044 in accordance with the rules of the Order of Saint Clare, a contemplative community of the Catholic Church.

The renowned poet, T. S. Eliot, demonstrates a profound understanding of a calling with these words:

> With the drawing of this Love, and the voice of this Calling, we shall not cease from exploration and the end of all our exploring will be to arrive where we started and know the place for the first time. (1971)

Much of our life is devoted to the search for the true self, the self that is committed to and engaged in the activity that matters most to us. When we find it we know it and the search is over. It is then we realize what we've been seeking is ourself, something we've always had with us but hidden by distractions.

Postscript

In 2019 the Little Star Foundation had its tax exempt status revoked, encouraging skeptics of Jaeger's altruism to question her standing as a true philanthropist.

Questions

A severe shoulder injury contributed to Jaeger's retirement from professional tennis. Does this make her charitable work less commendable?

Is the life chosen by Pennefather a life that provides no benefit to others and is therefore a wasted life?

6. Eric Liddell: Observing the Sabbath

God made me fast. And when I run, I feel his pleasure.

- Eric Liddell

The unofficial titles "world's greatest athlete," "world's strongest man," and "world's fastest human" are given to Olympic gold medalists in the decathlon, weightlifting, and 100 meter sprint respectively. Eric Liddell represented Great Britain in the 1924 Summer Olympic Games held in Paris. Liddell, a sprinter, had set the British record in the 100 yard dash at 9.7 seconds the previous year and was favored to win the gold medal and title "world's fastest human." But he chose not to run in the race that might have given him this sobriquet. Before boarding the ship for Paris Liddell was aware the qualifying heat for the 100 meter sprint would be held on a Sunday. A devout Christian, he refused to compete on the Sabbath, citing the fourth commandment:

> Six days shalt thou labour, and do all thy work.
> Remember the Sabbath day, to keep it holy.
> But the seventh day is the Sabbath of the LORD thy God: in it thou shalt not do any work, thou, nor thy son, nor thy daughter, nor thy manservant, nor thy maidservant, nor thy cattle, nor thy stranger that is within thy gates: For in six days He created heaven and earth, the sea, and all that in them is, and rested the seventh day: wherefore the LORD blessed the Sabbath day, and hallowed it. (Exodus 20:8-11, King James Version)

One of the ways by which we can know ourselves is our significant decisions, especially those that required sacrifice. Liddell's sacrifice of

23

an opportunity for a gold medal in the 100 meter sprint and recognition as the "world's fastest human" certainly reinforced his identity as a committed Christian. His decision is similar to baseball legend Sandy Koufax's decision not to pitch the first game of the 1965 World Series. Koufax, who is Jewish, famously chose not to play baseball on Yom Kippur, the holiest of the Judaism's holy days, a day of repentance and atonement. He went on pitch three times in the series, twice shutting out the Minnesota Twins including the decisive seventh game won by the Dodgers 2-0. Like Koufax, Liddell eventually competed in other events. In the Paris Olympics he won the bronze medal in the 200 meter race and gold medal in the 400 meter run, setting a world record in the latter.

Liddell served as a Christian missionary in China from 1926 to 1945. During World War II he was interned in a Japanese prison camp where he died at age 43 from a brain tumor. A Scotsman, he became the subject of a research project carried out by Charles Walker, a fellow Scotsman, who was determined to find the unmarked grave of Eric Liddell. "I was working on a book about Scots, and the more I talked to people who had known Liddell," said Walker, "the more convinced we all became that his grave should be marked." (Basler, 1990). "Armed with notes from the former prisoners and an old map of the area … the little camp grave-yard was still intact …marked only with small wooden crosses, but people present at (Liddell's) funeral recalled which was Mr. Liddell's." (1990)

A granite marker now stands over his grave with a brief biography in English and Chinese. It includes a quotation from the Old Testament prophetic book of Isaiah: "They shall mount up with wings as eagles; they shall run, and not be weary." (Isaiah 40:31, English Standard Version) An Academy Award winning movie, *Chariots of Fire*, tells the story of Liddell's commitment and accomplishments. (1981)

Question

Is Eric Liddell an example of extraordinary faith or religious fanaticism?

7. Kerri Strug: Taking One for the Team

We all have dreams. But in order to make dreams come into reality, it takes an awful lot of determination, dedication, self-discipline, and effort.

- Jesse Owens

The ones who are successful are the ones who really want it. You have to have that inner drive otherwise it's not going to work out.

- Kerri Strug

One of the most memorable moments in Olympic Games history occurred in 1996 when an 18-year-old, 4'8" gymnast named Kerri Strug completed her pommel horse vault by landing on a severely injured ankle. The injury, later diagnosed as a third degree lateral sprain with tendon damage, had occurred in her previous vault. Courageous? Of course it was. Yet Strug's heroic, gold medal winning performance is even more impressive as a demonstration of self-discipline.

Self-discipline is the capacity for doing the harder thing, enabling an individual to do what ought to be done, when it ought to be done regardless of inhibiting feelings. Arguably, the impulse to avoid pain is the strongest inhibitor to human action. However, neuroscientist Robert Sapolsky has written about the effect of emotion on the brain's interpretation of and response to pain:

> The emotional/interpretive level can be dissociated from the objective amount of pain signal that is coursing up to the brain from the spine. In other words, how much pain you feel, and how you feel, and how unpleasant that pain feels, can be two separate things (2004, pp. 193-194).

When contemplating an action or resisting an impulse the brain's frontal cortex provides a menu of possible outcomes, as well as the probability of each. This assessment is followed by a question: *Are you certain you want to do this?* Imagine Kerri Strug's frontal cortex operating at full-force while performing her vault, relentlessly informing her of the intense pain awaiting her when she would land on her injured ankle from a height exceeding her own. Further imagine the self-discipline required for her to stay on task, concentrating on her form while her frontal cortex was franticly advising her against what she was doing. The mind, the entity that directs mental processing, is capable of overruling the frontal cortex.

Kerri's heroic vault did not go unrecognized. She visited the White House to be congratulated by President Clinton, was featured on the cover of *Sports Illustrated*, and appeared on a box of Wheaties. In 2000 she was inducted into the International Jewish Sports Hall of Fame.

Question

Was it wrong for Bela Karolyi, Kerri's coach, to insist that she perform one more vault in spite of her severely injured ankle?

8. Archibald "Moonlight" Graham: Field of Dreams

You must give up the life you planned in order to have the life that is waiting for you.

- Joseph Campbell

If the name "Moonlight" Graham has a ring of familiarity it's because you've seen the feel good movie *Field of Dreams*, based on the W. B. Kinsella novel, *Shoeless Joe*. Given this story's mixture of fictional and real life characters it would be understandable to think of Graham as the product of Kinsella's imagination. But Archibald Graham actually played major league baseball for two innings in 1905. Called up from the minor leagues to the National League New York Giants he played right field in the eighth and ninth innings of a game on June 29, 1905. He neither fielded a ball nor had an at bat. (He was on deck to hit when the third out of the ninth inning was made.)

Returned to the minors later that season, he played three more years without returning to the big leagues. While continuing to play he prepared for life after baseball by enrolling in medical college at the University of Maryland, graduating in 1908. With his M.D. he settled in Chisholm, Minnesota where he practiced for 50 years, retiring in 1959. There he was appreciated and respected as the kind and generous family physician in Chisholm, a city with a population of 7,500. In the movie when his two inning major league career is referred to as a tragedy he responds, "Son, if I'd only gotten to be a doctor for five minutes now that would have been a tragedy." (1989)

While the common wisdom is "never give up on your dream" psychoanalyst Adam Phillip believes it is wise to abandon some aspirations. "What was not possible," he writes, "all too easily becomes the story of our lives. Our lives might become a protracted mourning for, or an endless trauma about, the lives we were unable to live." (2013, p. 77) Writer Judith Viorst also advocates giving up on some dreams in the interest of growth. In *Necessary Losses* she writes,

> We must confront, in the dreams we dream, as well as in our intimate relationships, all that we will never have and never will be. Passionate investment leaves us vulnerable to loss. And sometimes, no matter how clever we are, we must lose. (1986, p. 161)

The stories of those who refused to give up on a dream and made it come true are the stuff of which inspirational books and movies are made. In contrast, the stories of those who wisely gave up on a dream to pursue other goals usually go untold. Ordinary lives do not provide material for inspiring, motivational stories. Were it not for Kinsella's curiosity and research few of us would know about "Moonlight" Graham. We can't all be contenders. This realization led Graham to opt for a satisfying, albeit little-known, life. A half-century of residents of Chisholm benefitted from his choice. As for his dream of playing major league baseball, philosopher David Elton Trueblood submits, "Our deepest tragedy ... is not the tragedy of failing to realize our dream but that of not even having the dream." (1951, p. 130).

Question

Is it an unwise teaching to "never give up on a dream?"

9. Eddie Waitkus: The Natural?

Show me a hero and I'll write you a tragedy.

- F. Scott Fitzgerald

Bernard Malamud's novel, *The Natural*, spawned the movie with the same name, starring Robert Redford and Glenn Close. The story is the interrupted baseball career of Roy Hobbs, whose ability to hit a baseball borders on superhuman. The interruption occurred when an admiring fan, an emotionally disturbed woman, attempts to kill him by shooting him in a Chicago hotel room. Hobbs survives but his career is nearly derailed by a lengthy recovery and rehabilitation.

Roy Hobbs is fictional, the product of Malamud's imagination. Eddie Waitkus is not. On June 14, 1949 in a Chicago hotel room Waitkus was shot by Ruth Ann Steinhagen, an emotionally disturbed woman who was obsessed with him. She lured him into her hotel room with the note she left for him at the front desk:

> It's extremely important that I see you as soon as possible. We're not acquainted but I have something of importance to speak to you about. I think it would be to your advantage to let me explain it to you. Please come soon. I won't take much of your time. (Edelman, 2022)

Waitkus, a first baseman for the Philadelphia Phillies, had played for the Chicago Cubs before being traded. The Phillies were in Chicago playing the Cubs. The trade devastated Steinhagen, who felt she had lost this man she admired from afar. Waitkus nearly died from being shot in the chest with her 22 caliber rifle. She had planned to commit suicide after killing him but claimed she was unable to find another bullet. (In the movie the woman who shot Hobbes commits suicide.)

When survival is uncertain playing baseball is unimportant. Remarkably, 17 months after the shooting Waitkus returned to baseball, playing all 154 games for the 1950 National League pennant winning Philadelphia Phillies and four games in the World Series against the New York Yankees. Of course he was named baseball's Comeback Player of the Year. Waitkus, who went on to play five more seasons, died of esophageal cancer at age 53.

In Waitkus' biography his son, Ted, makes an arresting observation. When his father was rehabilitating in Clearwater Beach, Florida after the shooting he met Carol Webel, who he would eventually marry. Now an attorney in Colorado, Ted reflected that if his father had not been shot he would not exist.

Of course, speculation abounds as to whether Eddie Waitkus inspired Malamud's Roy Hobbs. (Malamud never confirmed the relationship, the striking similarities notwithstanding.) What is not subject to speculation is Waitkus' love of baseball and resilience. In the Cambridge High and Latin School class of 1937 yearbook it is written of him, "He'd like to play baseball without end. For baseball is a real good friend." (Theodore, 2002).

Question

The woman who shot Eddie did not go to prison but a psychiatric hospital where she was released after three years and lived the rest of her life in relative anonymity. Was this a miscarriage of justice?

10. Dave Dravecky: When You Can't Come Back

To have a comeback, you have to have a setback.

- Laurence Tureaud ("Mr. T")

Jim Abbott was a major league pitcher in spite of being born without a right hand. Pete Gray was a major league outfielder in spite of having his right arm amputated as the result of a childhood accident. Shaquem Griffin played in the National Football League as a linebacker in spite of a birth defect that resulted in his left hand being amputated when he was four-years-old. And then there is Dave Dravecky.

Dravecky was a left-handed pitcher for the San Diego Padres (1982-1987) and San Francisco Giants (1987-1989). He won 64 games in his eight year career with a creditable 3.13 earned run average and pitched two scoreless innings in the 1983 Major League All Star Game. In 1988 a cancerous tumor was found in his pitching arm. The tumor was surgically removed along with half of his deltoid (shoulder) muscle. Remarkably, ten months later he returned to the Giants and pitched eight innings in a 4-3 win over the Cincinnati Reds. Five days later, pitching against the Montreal Expos, he broke the bone in his upper left arm. The sound of the break was heard throughout the stadium. The cancer had returned.

Two more surgeries followed to excise the malignant tumor. When they failed, a third surgery was performed in the spring of 1991 amputating his left arm and shoulder. The irony of losing the arm that provided his livelihood is striking. He described the work he loved and lost with these words:

All you have to do is pick up a baseball. It begs to you: throw me. If you took a year to design an object to hurl, you'd end up with that little spheroid small enough to nestle in your fingers but big enough to have some heft, lighter than a rock but heavier than a hunk of wood. Its even, neat stitching, laced into the leather's slippery white surface, gives your fingers a purchase. A baseball was made to throw. It's almost irresistible. (01/18/2022)

Dave's Christian faith is evident from his reflection on life after baseball. "When I broke my arm, I knew there was something a lot bigger than baseball (about to happen) … I had a sense that God had something for me, something bigger than baseball." (01/19/2022). He's not bitter about the loss of his arm. In an interview 27 years after the amputation he said despite or maybe because of his cancer he enjoys life each day. (Strumpfer, 2018) The self-proclaimed "One-Armed Bandit" travels the country as a motivational and inspirational speaker. With his wife, Jan, he established "Endurance," a ministry that helps cancer patients deal with loss and depression.

Dave Dravecky exemplifies an analysis made by the journalist Norman Cousins, "Free will and determinism are like a game of cards. The hand that is dealt you is determinism. The way you play your hand is free will." (2022)

Question

Some philosophers maintain heroism requires a choice. Did Dave have no choice but to reinvent himself?

11. Aron Ralston and Ben Comen: On Cutting and Running

If you can force your heart and nerve and sinew
To serve their turn long after they are gone
And so hold on when there is nothing left in you
Except the will which says to them "hold on."

- Rudyard Kipling

In 2003 columnist Rick Reilly wrote two stories that appeared in *Sports Illustrated* within weeks of each other. The first described a press conference at which a 28 year-old mountaineer named Aron Ralston spoke about the self-amputation of his right arm. The second featured Ben Comen, a South Carolina high school cross-country runner who has finished last in every race in which he has competed. Ben Comen has cerebral palsy. Aron Ralston and Ben Comen not only exemplify perseverance, they are exemplary of it.

When my daughter was a little girl, we played a game with language. I would say to her, "Rachel Joy, say something that no one ever said before." She would respond with statements like, "Stop eating that bus!" and, "Can you juggle your ears?" I thought of that game when I first heard about Aaron Ralston. I'm guessing he was the first person to say "I cut off my right arm with a utility knife."

Trapped in a Utah cave when an 800-pound boulder shifted and pinned his arm against the cave's wall, after five days of futility he decided to do the only thing that could save his life. Neither his self-surgery nor his description of it was delicate. At the press conference he described the three step procedure of cutting (flesh, muscle, and tendons), breaking (ulna and radius bones), and snipping (nerve). Weakened by a 45 pound weight loss, Ralston accomplished the amputation that saved his life.

As an athlete Ben Comen has provided us with a riddle: How could America's slowest high school cross country runner also be the best known? The answer is when he is featured in *Sports Illustrated* because of his persistence. Cerebral palsy is a congenital disorder of the central nervous system characterized by spastic paralysis and defective motor functioning. Ben's cerebral palsy does not impair him intellectually (he is an excellent student), but it has a devastating effect on his cross country time. Unable to complete the three-mile course without falling numerous times and impaired in his ability to get up after falling, his 50-minute performances placed him last in every race he ran. Typically, the first-place time in a high school meet is between 16 and 19 minutes for boys. Ben always finished 20 minutes behind the second from last runner. But he always finished!

In addition to crossing the finish line with cuts and abrasions Ben was accompanied by admiring teammates who ran back to join him after they completed the course. Spectators knew the race was not over until Ben crossed the finish line and waited for him, all applauding, some cheering, and a few crying.

Motivation is the inner drive that initiates and sustains activity. Like the wind, it is a force that cannot be seen and is inferred from its effect. Aron Ralston's motivation was to survive. Ben Comen's motivation is not as obvious. Perhaps Ben perseveres to experience the exhilaration that comes from prevailing in a challenge. Each in his own way serves as an illustration of extraordinary persistence. Aron Ralston is to be admired because he took control in his circumstances. At his press conference he said after days of despair it actually felt good to realize that he could do something. Convinced he was going to die and not knowing when his body would be found, he etched his name into the wall of the cave for the purpose of identification. Ironically, it was when he used his knife for his epitaph that it occurred to him he could also use it to free himself. He was encouraged and energized by the realization that the 800-pound boulder would not determine the time and place of his death.

In Aron Ralston's memoir, appropriately titled, *Between a Rock and a Hard Place*, he describes an inventory he took before severing his arm. He considered the things he enjoyed and concluded only piano playing required both his arms.

Similarly, Ben Comen fought back. His adversary was not a boulder but a formidable disease. Like Aron, he resolved not to be held in place. Avoidance of pain is a primal human impulse. Both of these young men pushed through pain to achieve something they valued. They move us to ask what we value enough to push through pain.

Question

What accounts for the extraordinary perseverance shown by Aron and Ben?

12.   The Green Bay Packers and Dallas Cowboys: The Ice Bowl

Men wanted for a hazardous journey. Small wages. Bitter cold. Long months of complete darkness. Constant danger. Safe return doubtful. Honour and recognition in case of success!

- Ernest Shackleton

In 1914, twenty-seven men responded to Ernest Shackleton's call for crewman to join an expedition that would be the first to cross Antarctica. Shackleton's foreboding advertisement proved to be understated. Their ship sunk and they endured unspeakable pain as castaways in one of the world's most hostile and frigid environments.

On December 31, 1967 the Green Bay Packers and Dallas Cowboys played for the National Football League Championship in a game that came to be known as the Ice Bowl. To equate a football game with the Shackleton expedition would be preposterous. Nevertheless, there is value in learning about the greatest display of endurance ever shown on a football field.

"It was as cold as I'll ever be in my life; I'll never be that cold again." (1997) With these words Dallas Cowboys safety Mel Renfro spoke for players, coaches, referees, and 50,000 spectators who endured three hours in Lambeau Field for a football game played in minus 14 degree weather with a wind chill factor of minus 46. By the game's end, the wind chill had dipped to 69 below zero.

The determination to continue at a task through pain and fatigue is admirable. At one time or another we all have experienced the pain of cold. The philosopher René Descartes explained pain as injured nerves sending impulses to the brain - analogous to pulling a rope to ring a bell. However, "Pain is a property not only of the senses of the region where we feel it - but of the brain as well." (Myers, 2004, p. 221) In fact, the brain can create pain without injured nerves. In phantom limb pain there is no rope to be pulled. Also, the brain records experiences as painful, making it unnecessary to recreate the sensation of pain. Fortunately, we do not have to re-experience the pain of being burned in order to be careful around fire. It is the memory of that painful day that enabled Dallas fullback Don Perkins to say, "Wow, that was one cold mother." (1997)

Listening to the stories of those who were there provide us with an appreciation of how cold it was. Television commentator Frank Gifford was incredulous when his 6:00 am hotel wakeup call greeted him with, "Good morning Mr. Gifford, the temperature is minus 29 degrees - the coldest New Year's Eve in Green Bay history." Later that day, in the unheated press box, Gifford put a cup of coffee to his lips, realized the coffee had frozen, and said, "It looks like I'm going to have a bite of coffee." (1997) Two other Ice Bowl stories involving lips are the cancellation of the halftime show and referees not using their whistles. When a musician's lip got stuck to his instrument it was decided to forego halftime entertainment. Similarly, on the first play of the game, when a referee pulled his whistle from his mouth his lip began bleeding. "It bled only for a moment," recalled Cowboys' tackle Bob Lilly, "and then the blood froze almost immediately on his chin." (1997)

Under normal conditions the body heat generated by playing is sufficient to keep players warm. But this game was not played under normal conditions. Green Bay guard Jerry Kramer recalled it as the only time he did not eventually warm up from playing. Like the weather, he got colder and colder as the afternoon progressed.

All the players' efforts to get warmer met with futility. Dallas wide receiver Lance Rentzel recounted that some of his teammates wrapped their feet in saran wrap believing that cellophane could resist cold and retain heat. Renfro recalled there were butane heaters on the sidelines that the players huddled around when they came off the field. The smell of burning rubber alerted some of them that their shoes were melting. Their numb feet had made them unaware of their self-inflicted hot foot.

Cold feet were not the only problem. Packers' linebacker Dave Robinson concealed his disobedience to Coach Vince Lombardi's insistence that his players not wear gloves. Robinson, who is Black, wore brown gloves, telling the equipment manager, "He (Coach Lombardi) won't know the difference" (1997). Cold hands neutralized the Cowboy's most dangerous and exciting player, Bob Hayes. Nicknamed "The Bullet," Hayes had won the Gold Medal in the 100 meter dash in the 1964 Olympics. Early in the game the Green Bay defense noted that Hayes tucked his hands in the waistband of his pants if he was being used as a decoy. When a passing play called for him as a receiver he lined up with his hands on his hips. On that day the world's fastest human was the world's coldest wide receiver.

Faces were also a concern. Late in the game Dallas quarterback Don Meredith was unintelligible to his teammates when he tried to call a play in the huddle. It was only after one of them quickly massaged Meredith's frozen face that he could be understood.

The playing field was frozen, making it more like an ice-skating rink than a football field. Packers' fullback Chuck Mercein described getting tackled, "like falling on jagged concrete." (1997) Renfro remembered it as, "Jagged ice…that was like taking a razor to your jersey." (1997) Rentzel spoke of the eeriness of being on the field and hearing thousands of spectators who could not be seen because of their vaporized breath. "There was this incredible haze of breath," writes journalist David Maraniss, "Tens of thousands of puffs coming out. Like seeing big buffaloes in an enormous herd on the winter plains. It was prehistoric." (1999, p. 416) Rentzel said it was surreal.

The Green Bay Packers scored the winning touchdown with sixteen seconds remaining in the game. Their 21-17 victory made them no more admirable than the team they defeated. Packer offensive tackle Forrest Gregg estimated, "It's impossible to ask more of a group of players than was asked of them that day." (1997)

Endurance is the ability to stand up under pain, distress, or fatigue. Ironically, "Endurance" was the name of Ernest Shackleton's ship. It is also the word that accurately describes the players and spectators who braved the bone-rattling cold that made this game the Ice Bowl.

Questions

Should this game have been postponed?

Should the Packers and Cowboys players have refused to play this game?

STORIES THAT RAISE A MORAL QUESTION

There are four criteria that make an issue a moral issue. Moral issues involve:

1. a clear question of right vs. wrong conduct
2. a generally recognized moral principle
3. consequences for at least one person other than the decision-maker
4. the assumption of responsibility

Each of the stories in this next section imply an ethical issue. In each case there's either an absence of a clear moral guideline or a guideline that is questionable.

13.   A Barlett Giamatti: On Cheating

The one constant through all the years Ray, has been baseball. America has rolled by like an army of steamrollers. It's been erased like a blackboard, rebuilt and erased again. But baseball has marked the time. This field, this game, is a part of our past, Ray. It reminds us of all that once was good, and that could be again.

- James Earl Jones as Terrance Mann in *Field of Dreams*

No sport has ever had a more academically accomplished commissioner than Major League Baseball when its commissioner was A. Bartlett Giamatti. A Professor of English Renaissance Literature, he became the youngest President of Yale University, his alma mater, at the age of 40. However, his passion for baseball prevailed over his love for higher education and in 1986 he accepted the positon of President of the National League, which he held for three years before his election as Commissioner of Major League Baseball. His untimely death from a heart attack five months later prematurely ended what likely would have been an exceptional tenure as professional baseball's chief executive.

While serving as National League President Giamatti ruled on an appeal made on behalf of Kevin Gross, a Philadelphia Phillies pitcher who had attached a piece of sandpaper to his glove in order to secretively scuff the baseball. (Scuffing a ball affects its movement making it more difficult to hit.) This is an unquestionable rule violation. Gross was ejected from the game and suspended for ten days. The suspension was appealed, requiring Giamatti to reconsider the suspension. Of his decision he said,

I worked as hard on my response to the Kevin Gross Appeal as I worked on anything I did while I was in New Haven (at Yale University). It was challenging to try to be clear about cheating and what it meant, and to be fair at the same time. (Robson, 1998, p. 66).

The basis of the appeal was, "the ten-day suspension was unduly harsh; it was without precedent, inconsistent with past practices, and not comparable with discipline for other offenses." (p. 68) In his written decision, Giamatti brilliantly made a distinction between an act of premeditated cheating and a spontaneous loss of control.

There is a category of offenses and discipline that involve cheating. Such acts are not the result of impulse, borne of frustration or anger or zeal as violence is, but rather are acts of a cool, deliberate, premeditated kind. Unlike acts of impulse or violence, intended at the moment to vent frustration or abuse another, acts of cheating are intended to alter the very conditions of play to favor one person. They are secretive, covert acts that strike at and seek to undermine the basic foundation of any contest declaring the winner - that all participants play under identical rules and conditions. Acts of cheating destroy that necessary foundation and thus strike at the essence of a contest. They destroy faith in the games' integrity and fairness; if participants and spectators alike cannot assume integrity and fairness, and proceed from there, the contest in its essence cannot exist.

Acts of physical excess, reprehensible as they are, often represent extensions of the very forms of physical exertion that are the basis for playing the game; regulation and discipline seek to contain, not expunge, violent effort in sports. Cheating, on the other hand, has no organic basis in the game and no origins in the act of playing. Cheating is contrary to the whole purpose of playing to determine a winner fairly and cannot be simply contained; if the game is to flourish and engage public confidence, cheating must be clearly condemned with an eye to expunging it. (Robson, 1998, pp. 72-73)

Could there be a more eloquent description of the difference between cheating and an impulsive loss of control? Could there be a more eloquent argument for the importance of fair play?

Question

Do you agree with Giamatti that cheating is a more serious offense than a violent act resulting from a loss of control while competing?

14. Denny McLain: One for the Mick

I'm gonna let him hit one.

- Denny McLain

A. Bartlett Giamatti's eloquent condemnation of cheating notwithstanding, there's something heartwarming about Denny McLain breaking the rules in an inconsequential baseball game. By September 19, 1968 the Detroit Tigers had clinched the American League pennant. They were in the last week of a 103 win season and looking forward to taking on the St. Louis Cardinals in the World Series. In contrast, the once mighty New York Yankees were languishing in sixth place looking forward to the end of their dismal season.

Similar to his team, the once mighty Yankee icon Mickey Mantle was finishing up his last season with statistics that bore no resemblance to the seasons of his youth. His 18 home runs in 1968 were far distant from the 52 he hit in 1956 and 54 in 1961. His anemic .237 batting average was 128 points lower than his .365 a dozen years earlier. But there's something to be said about longevity and after 18 seasons "The Mick" had accumulated 534 home runs as of September 19, 1968, placing him tied for third on baseball's all-time home run list. He was tied with the long retired Jimmy Foxx and well behind the seemingly unapproachable Babe Ruth (714 home runs) and still active Willie Mays (587 home runs).

All of the above sets the stage for the eighth inning of the aforementioned inconsequential game between the Tigers and Yankees. In the top of the eighth with the Tigers leading 6-1 with their ace on the mound the Yankees had the appearance of the Mudville nine

49

immortalized in Ernest Thayer's classic poem. Denny McLain, the Tigers' pitcher, was en route to a 31 win season and both the Cy Young and Most Valuable Player awards. (Mantle had won the Most Valuable Player award three times.) Mantle was warmly received by the Tigers fans knowing this would be his last at bat in Briggs Stadium.

> When Mantle came to bat in the eighth inning, Denny McLain walked off the mound to allow him to bask in the standing ovation offered by the meager crowd. Mantle was his hero, the reason he became a switch hitter in high school. McLain had already won his thirtieth game of the year, becoming the first pitcher since Dizzy Dean to do so. He could afford to be magnanimous. (Leavy, 2010, p. 285).

McLain called his catcher, Jim Price, to the mound and said, "Listen, he only needs one home run. Let's give him a shot at it. You just go behind home plate, put up your glove, and let me see if I can hit it" (p. 285). The first pitch was neither a fastball nor a curve. It had no movement and moved plateward at 50 miles an hour, one-half the speed McLain was capable of throwing. In baseball parlance it was a batting practice pitch. Mantle took it for a strike, but recognized McLain's generosity. When Mantle fouled off the next pitch an exasperated McLain called out to Mantle, "Where the hell do you want it?" (p. 285). The next pitch came in where Mantle had indicated with his bat and the ball landed in the right field seats. As Mantle rounded third base he said to McLain, "Thank you, thank you. I owe ya, I owe ya." (p. 285)

Predictably, after the game McLain was cross-examined by sports writers who believed his kindness impugned the integrity of the game. Moreover, they questioned Mantle's right to third place on the all-time home run list. Baseball Commissioner William Eckert sent a letter to McLain threatening an investigation into the incident. Perhaps the legendary sportswriter Red Smith provided the most apt observation of the event when he wrote, "When a guy has bought 534 drinks in the same saloon, he's entitled to one on the house." (P. 286).

Postscript

The next day Mantle hit his 536th and last major league home run at Yankee Stadium. He received no help from the Red Sox pitcher, Jim Lonborg.

Question

Is cheating ever acceptable, even when it is motivated by kindness and has no effect on the outcome of the game?

15. James Braddock: The Bargain

Boxing is a great sport but a lousy business.

- Ken Norton

A little known but stunning instance of a man accommodating to the reality of his time is boxing legend Joe Louis. In 1937 he made an agreement to fight James Braddock for the heavyweight championship of the world. Louis was in line to fight the champion Braddock, also known as the "Cinderella Man," for professional sports' most coveted title. Braddock seemed to accept the probability that he would lose the title. Louis' record was 31 wins and one loss, with 27 of those wins coming by way of knockouts. Three of his knockouts were against former heavyweight champions (Primo Carnera, Max Baer, and Jack Sharkey). Braddock had the option of defending his title against a German contender named Max Schmeling, who had defeated Louis a year earlier by knocking him out in the 12th round of their fight.

Convinced he would lose the title to one or the other Braddock was determined to maximize his earnings from his last fight as champion. He preferred Louis as an opponent because he was a rising star in spite of his loss to Schmeling and would provide a bigger payday. Also, Braddock and Louis knew if Schmeling won the title Adolf Hitler would not allow him to risk the title in a rematch with the dangerous Black challenger Louis. Braddock offered to fight Louis if Louis would agree to give him ten percent of his earnings from title defenses for the next ten years. Louis agreed to Braddock's proposal, knowing if Schmeling wrested the title from Braddock he would not have an opportunity to fight for the title as long as Schmeling held it.

On June 22, 1937 Louis knocked out Braddock in the 8th round starting his 11 year reign as heavyweight champion of the world. Louis defended the title 25 times between 1937 and 1948 before retiring in 1949. Braddock earned $320,000 for his fight with Louis and approximately $150,000 in the ten years that followed. One defense was a first round knockout of Schmeling exactly one year to the day after winning the title. The match drew 70,000 spectators at Yankee Stadium and produced approximately $1,000,000 in gate receipts. A conservative estimate is James Braddock earned $50,000 that night without giving or taking a single punch.

Questions

Was Braddock's offer a favor to Louis or was Braddock taking unfair advantage of him?

Did Louis compromise by accepting Braddock's offer?

16.   Harry Haft: Fighting for His Life

Arbeit macht frei
(Work makes you free.)
> - sign over the entrance gate to Auschwitz

Literally, Harry Haft fought for his life. A Polish Jew, he was imprisoned in Auschwitz, the largest of the Nazi concentration and extermination camps. There he earned a modicum of special privileges by winning boxing matches. The sadistic fights were held for the entertainment of prison guards and German soldiers. Although he had never boxed before Auschwitz, Haft acquired the nickname "The Jewish Animal" from the beatings he administered to fellow prisoners who were no match for him. To win meant a sip of whiskey, a few bites of solid food or temporary relief from hard labor. To lose meant a walk to the gas chambers and cremation in an oven. That he lived to escape from captivity in 1945 is proof that he was undefeated.

It would be understandable if Haft never again fought after he became a free man. Instead, he became a professional boxer after emigrating to the United States in 1948. He competed as a light heavyweight and heavyweight, weighing approximately 175 pounds. His incentive for fighting was not survival but the hope that he would be reunited with Leah, the woman he loved and planned to marry before they were taken in the Holocaust. He didn't know if she had survived or, literally, where in the world she was if she did. His hope was if he could become a world champion she would hear about him and find him.

Harry made a good start toward his goal, winning his first twelve fights. But in the way that professional boxing works, he moved up to face more challenging opponents and began losing. His last fight sent him into retirement and ended his dream of reuniting with Leah. Eventual world heavyweight champion Rocky Marciano easily disposed of Haft in three rounds. Still, Harry Haft is to be appreciated for his determination to survive and pursue the life he might have had.

Question

Should Harry have refused to entertain his captors by engaging in fights to the death?

17. Jake LaMotta: Does the End Justify the Means?

There's only one thing I wanted out of life and that was to be the champ.

- Jake LaMotta

The principle "the end justifies the means" originated with Niccolo Machiavcelli's *The Prince*, written in the 16th century. Applications of this concept have gone well beyond his intention, which offers guidance in a specific, rarefied situation. Nevertheless, it has come to mean an action is morally right if it achieves the desired goal. It is this understanding, unintended by Machiavelli, that is brought to a 1947 boxing match between Jake LaMotta and "Blackjack" Billy Fox.

If accomplishment determines worthiness for a title fight then LaMotta would have been next in line to fight for the middleweight championship of the world, then held by Marcel Cerdan. But such was not the case in post-Prohibition boxing.

> When prohibition came to end in 1933, after more than a decade of lucrative and bloody endeavor for the Mob, they needed something new. Access to the machinery of boxing, a willfully unfettered anarchy still ripe for abuse today, proved remarkably easy to acquire. (Payne, 2020).

In 1947 organized crime figures controlled not only who would fight but who would win. Some fighters, like Rocky Marciano and Carmen Basilio, managed to resist cooperating with the Mafia. Others, like Jake LaMotta, resisted until it prevented an opportunity to fight for a title and the earnings that came with it.

It wasn't cowardice. It wasn't even the money. It was the only way. The only way to get my shot. What was mine, I'd earned it. Nobody would give me a chance. Five years as the uncrowned champion. I deserved that shot. I did what needed to be done. (2020)

LaMotta's predicament raises the question of moral conduct in a corrupt system. Five months before the Fox fight LaMotta turned down money to lose to Tony Janiro, who he beat in a ten round unanimous decision. Finally, in exchange for an opportunity to fight Cerdan, he not only agreed to lose to Fox but paid $20,000 to secure the deal. Throwing the fight did not come easily for LaMotta, who recalled:

The first round, a couple of belts to his head, and I see a glassy look coming over his eyes. Jesus Christ, a couple of jabs and he's going to fall down? I began to panic a little. I was supposed to be throwing a fight to this guy, and it looked like I was going to end up holding him on his feet... By [the fourth round], if there was anybody in the Garden who didn't know what was happening, he must have been dead drunk. (Merron, 2008)

Fox's record prior to fighting LaMotta was impressive. He had won his first 38 professional fights by knocking out opponents far less capable than LaMotta. On November 14, 1947, to the surprise of no one in the Mob, Fox defeated LaMotta by a fourth round technical knockout. As promised, LaMotta got his fight with Cerdan who he defeated to become the middleweight champion of the world.

A Sad Postscript

The rematch that was scheduled for later that same year never happened. On October 28, 1949 Cerdan boarded an ill-fated airliner headed for New York City where he planned to spend time with his lover, the famous singer Edith Piaf. The plane crashed on an island in the Azores killing all 48 passengers.

Question

Is Jake guilty of a moral failure by throwing the fight?

18. Billy Miske: Dead Man Fighting

You can take all your Tiny Tims and your Grinches and your Miracles on Whatever Street and stuff them in your stocking. The best Christmas story is about a boxer.

- Rick Reilly

To say Billy Miske was tough would be an understatement. He boxed as a light heavyweight and heavyweight from 1913 to 1923. His 105 fights included encounters with the best of his contemporaries, including two brawls with Jack Dempsey. Nicknamed "The St. Paul Thunderbolt," Billie's career came to halt in 1923, five years after being diagnosed with Bright's disease, a debilitating kidney condition now referred to as nephritis. When diagnosed he was told he had five years to live.

Also unfortunate for Billy was his alternative source of income was as failing as his kidneys. His car dealership in his hometown St. Paul, Minnesota had put him $100,000 in debt. As Christmas of 1923 approached Billy resorted to his only means for providing what he believed would be his last Christmas with his family.

Although too sick to train he contacted his manager, Jack Reddy, and asked him to arrange a fight. Reddy refused, reminding Billie that he's dying and a fight could kill him. Billy responded that he's going to die soon anyway and he has a plan for how he'd like to make his exit. Realizing he's arguing with a desperate man, Reddy arranged a match with Bill Brennan, a rugged heavyweight who himself had gone 12 rounds with Dempsey in a title fight.

On November 7, 1923 an ill prepared Billy stepped into the ring in Omaha, Nebraska. (He had been too ill to get out of bed to train for the fight.) Astonishingly he won the fight, knocking Brennan out in the fourth round. (Although Brennan was out of shape for the fight he was in far better condition than the almost dead man he fought.)

The $2,400 Billy earned financed the Miske family's last Christmas, a day of celebration with presents that included a baby grand piano, toys, new furniture, and a sumptuous dinner. There was enough money left over for Billy's wife, Marie, to put aside for the future. The following day Billy called Reddy to ask him to take him to the hospital. There he was persuaded to tell Marie about the illness he had kept from her. On the morning of the first day of 1924 Billy Miske died.

Tommy Gibbons, another boxer from St. Paul and, like Billy, inducted into the International Boxing Hall of Fame, said, "I always had the highest regard for Billy Miske, both as a boxer and a man. He gave me more trouble than any boxer I ever met, and that includes Jack Dempsey. Miske was a credit to boxing." (Moyle, 2012). He is also a credit to the human spirit, demonstrating what people are capable of even when terminally ill.

Question

Was Billy wrong to hasten his death by fighting one last fight?

19. Armando Gallaraga: The Imperfect Game

To err is human, to forgive is rare.

- Anonymous

On June 2, 2010, Armando Gallaraga, a pitcher for the Detroit Tigers, retired 26 consecutive Cleveland Indians. He appeared to have achieved the so-called perfect game in which no batter reaches base when the 27th Indian batter hit a routine ground ball fielded by the Tigers' first baseman and tossed to Gallaraga covering first base for the final out. The celebration of this rare event turned to amazement when first base umpire Jim Joyce made an obvious error and called the runner safe, depriving Gallaraga of what would have been the 23rd perfect game in major league baseball's 135 year history.

Unlike football, in 2010 baseball had no provision for a video tape review and reversal of an incorrect call by an umpire. When Joyce saw the replay after the game he admitted his error. The only person with the authority to overrule Joyce's call was the Commissioner of Major League Baseball, Bud Selig. He refused to do so, reasoning it would be the first time a Commissioner overturned an umpire's judgment call and would establish an unwise precedent. Selig's decision was consistent with a principle of jurisprudence: the law is concerned with neither right nor wrong – only precedent. Selig also admitted to a preference for video tape replays not being used in baseball.

I don't know how we could use it to improve the job that umpires do. The human element in sport has always been a big part of the game. I'm a football fan, too, and I hate instant replay in the NFL. Football games are taking four hours. (2022)

Nevertheless, in 2014 instant replay and reversal of an umpire's ruling was instituted in its current practice. (It had been experimented with and used on a limited basis starting in 2008.)

Was justice served by the Commissioner's decision? His critics argue that precedent should be set aside when it perpetuates an obvious injustice. Selig's supporters posit without strict adherence to precedent there is no reliable system for dispensing justice.

Postscript

In 2011 Armando Gallaraga, Jim Joyce, and Daniel Paisner collaborated on a book titled, *Nobody's Perfect: Two Men, One Call, and a Game for Baseball History.* (2011) Following the release of the book Major League Baseball did not allow Joyce to umpire any game in which Gallaraga would be playing to avoid any appearance of impropriety or conflict of interest.

Question

Was Commissioner Selig's decision not to overrule the umpire's call consistent with or contrary to justice?

20. Mike Tyson and Pete Rose: Halls of Fame

My whole life has been a waste – I've been a failure.

- Mike Tyson

The matter of Mr. Rose is now closed. It will be debated and discussed. Let no one think that it did not hurt baseball. That hurt will pass, however, as the great glory of the game asserts itself and a resilient institution goes forward. Let it also be clear that no individual is superior to the game.

- A. Bartlett Giamatti

Often, justice is not easily determined. Consider the following case of two great athletes, one of whom is in his sport's hall of fame and the other who is not.

On June 12, 2011 convicted rapist and former, self-proclaimed "Baddest Man on the Planet," Mike Tyson, was inducted into the International Boxing Hall of Fame. Twenty years earlier, on February 4, 1991, the governing body of the Baseball Hall of Fame determined that all names on major league baseball's permanently ineligible list were also permanently disqualified for consideration for enshrinement in Cooperstown. Pete Rose, who had played more games (3,562) and had more hits (4,256) than any other player in major league history, was on that list. Barring a change of heart and vote by that governing board, Pete Rose will never be inducted into the Baseball Hall of Fame.

Before pursuing whether this state of affairs is equitable, a cursory review of some history is in order. In 1992 Mike Tyson was convicted of raping an 18 year-old beauty pageant contestant, Desiree

Washington, in Indianapolis, Indiana. He subsequently served half of a six-year sentence before resuming his boxing career. This felony was hardly a blemish on an otherwise exemplary life. Other arrests and convictions preceded and followed the rape conviction. Further, even in the ring Tyson did not evade ignominy. In his 1997 fight with Evander Holyfield Tyson bit off one inch of Holyfield's ear in a third round clinch.

Two divorces would seem to disqualify Mike Tyson as a marriage counselor. His bankruptcy after having earned 300 million dollars over twenty years would seem to disqualify him as a financial advisor. However, being the youngest heavyweight champion in boxing history with an impressive record (50 wins in 58 fights, with 44 knockouts), entitles him to a place in boxing's Hall of Fame according to those entrusted with making this determination.

In August of 1989 the Commissioner of Major League Baseball, A. Bartlett Giamatti, and Pete Rose reached an agreement on the matter of Rose's gambling on baseball games and his future participation in the sport. At that time an ongoing investigation already had established that Rose had wagered on games in which he was involved when managing the Cincinnati Reds. (After denying he had bet on games, Rose eventually admitted to having done so, emphasizing that he never bet on the Reds to lose.) Giamatti agreed to discontinue the investigation if Rose would accept, without the option of appeal, his permanent ineligibility to participate in organized baseball.

Is it fair that Mike Tyson has the honor of hall of fame status and Pete Rose does not? This question cannot be addressed until two other questions are considered: What is justice? And, similarities notwithstanding, is likening Tyson and Rose an "apples to oranges" comparison?

What Is Justice?

Justice is the firm and continuous determination to render unto everyone that which is due. Retributive justice is concerned with determining penalties for transgressions. Often it is no easy matter to determine the appropriate punishment for an offense. The decision-makers for the International Boxing Hall of Fame determined that excluding Tyson owing to his criminal behavior outside of boxing would constitute an injustice. Commissioner Giamatti and the governing body of the Baseball Hall of Fame decided otherwise for Rose.

Has justice been served by one man receiving hall of fame recognition and the other being excluded? Is the only equitable determination of this honor the inductions of both or neither of these men? Has retributive justice been satisfied by Tyson's three-year incarceration for a criminal act and Rose's banishment for a rules violation? Is it defensible to claim that both men have been treated fairly?

Are These Two Cases Comparable?

It is tempting to compare the treatment these men have received from their respective sports. While it might be intuitive to claim that since Tyson has been inducted into his hall of fame, Rose should be inducted into his. Such an assertion is simplistic. Their situations are similar, but not identical. There are differences that justify Tyson's inclusion and Rose's exclusion.

There is nothing in the mission statement of the International Boxing Hall of Fame that precludes Mike Tyson's election: "Our mission is to honor and preserve boxing's rich heritage, chronicle the achievements of those who excelled and provide an educational experience for our many visitors." (International Boxing Hall of Fame.com)

Returning to the question of equanimity, the differences between these two cases are sufficient to conclude that comparing Tyson's to Rose's is an "apples to oranges" exercise. Undisputedly, raping a woman is more reprehensible than betting on a baseball game. Nevertheless, Tyson's offense was criminal and addressed accordingly. His debt was to society and he paid it. In contrast, Rose's transgression concerns only baseball and his punishment was determined by major league baseball's system for dealing with such matters. Responsible for maintaining the integrity of the game in accordance with his judgment, Commissioner Gamatti investigated Rose's activity and reached an agreement with him. Those advocating for Rose's admission into the Hall of Fame seem to disregard that he refused the opportunity to formally refute the charges against him. (True, the Hall of Fame's decision came two years after his refusal. However, Rose had no reason to believe that he ever would be removed from the ineligible list given the precedent set by Commissioner Kennesaw Mountain Landis when he banished "Shoeless" Joe Jackson in 1920.) In Commissioner Giamatti's statement to the press he described Rose's concession to permanent expulsion:

> The banishment for life of Pete Rose from baseball is the sad end of a sorry episode. One of the game's greatest players has engaged in a variety of acts which have stained the game, and he must now live with the consequences of those acts. By choosing not to come to a hearing before me, and by choosing not to offer any testimony or evidence contrary to the report of the special counsel to the commissioner, Mr. Rose has accepted baseball's ultimate sanction, lifetime ineligibility. (1998, p. 117)

Pete Rose disregarded baseball's most unambiguous rule and gambled that either he would not be discovered or, if discovered, it would not matter. Some of his apologists have pathetically argued that it doesn't matter what Rose did to injure the game; his statistics justify his place in Cooperstown. However, Rose's induction would declare that individual accomplishments trump all other considerations – including indifference to the sport's integrity. Other apologists have argued that Rose's personal life is unrelated to his professional life and should have no bearing on his participation in baseball. This is a strange argument given that he wagered on baseball games while professionally engaged in the sport. Mike Tyson never used either of these arguments to make a case for his Hall of Fame selection. In fact, he never claimed he deserved this honor and seemed surprised when it came.

Conclusion

Ultimately, the fairness of Tyson being "in" and Rose being "out" is a subjective judgment. For those who care enough about this issue to debate it, the position taken implies something about the one espousing it. This is true for anyone making a moral argument.

In closing, it's relevant to ask if more is expected of baseball players than boxers. "It ain't true, is it, Joe?" was not asked of Joe Louis, but Joe Jackson. The movie classic, *Field of Dreams*, based on W.P. Kinsella's novel, *Shoeless Joe*, includes Terrance Mann's eloquent oration in which baseball, not boxing, " ... reminds us of all that was good and could be again" (1982). Boxing has its devoted fans, but it does not have a place in the national heart in the way baseball does. Giamatti recognized this when he wrote:

It's designed to break your heart. The game begins in the spring, when everything is new again, and it blossoms in the summer, filling afternoons and evenings, and as soon as the chill rains come, it stops, and leaves you to face the fall alone. (1998, p. 121)

Questions

Is it an injustice to keep Pete Rose out of the Baseball hall of Fame?

Is it immoral for Mike Tyson to be in the International Boxing Hall of Fame?

References

Chapter 1

Rogers, F. (1992). Boston University Commencement. 05/17/1992. Nickerson Field. Boston, MA.

McRae, D. (2002). *Heroes Without a Country*. New York: Harper Collins, 2002).

Cannon, J. (1951*). The New York Post*. 10/26/1951.

Folsom, B. (1997). "Joe Louis vs. the IRS." Mackinac Center for Public Policy. Posted 06/07/1997. www.mackinac.org/article.05/21/2006.Retrieved 12/27/2021.

Chapter 2

Levy, A. (2008). *Floyd Patterson: A Boxer and a Gentleman*. Jefferson, NC: McFarland & Company, Inc. Publishers.

McRae, D. (1999). www.guardian.co.uk. 11/13/1999. Recovered on 12/25/2021.

Roosevelt, F.(2022). Recovered from www.gracious quotes.com>Leaders/Innovators on 02/17/2022.

Chapter 3

Trueblood, D. (1951). The life we prize. New York: Harper and Brothers.

Martin, D. (2012). "Jack Twyman, NBA star dies at 78." New York Times. 05/31/2012.

Chapter 4

Ali, M. (2021). Network warfare history. "Vietnam war: Muhammed Ali's draft controversy." The national interest. Retrieved 12/21/2021.

Dundee, A. (2012). "Dundee: Ali was, still is, the Greatest." ESPN 01/17/2012. Retrieved 12/21/2021.

King, M.L. (1998). *The Autobiography of Martin Luther King, Jr.* Clayborne Carson, editor. New York: Warner Books.

Metz, N. (2013). "The trials of a Chicago director making an Ali doc." *Chicago Tribune.* 08/31/2013. Retrieved on 12/22/2021.

Rhoden, W. (2013). "In Ali's voice from the past a standard for the ages." *New York Times.* 06/21/2013. Retrieved on 12/23/2021.

Whitcomb, D. (2016). "Former Ali promoter recall's boxer's impact on society." Reuters. 06/05/2016. Retrieved 12/24/2021.

Chapter 5

Berlet, B. (1995). "Seems it's Uconn's to lose." *Hartford Courant.* 03/03/1995.

Eliot, T.S. (1943). "Little gidding." Four quartets. New York: Houghton Mifflin Harcourt Publishing Co.

Chapter 6

Chariots of fire. (1981). Los Angeles, CA: 20th Century Fox.

Basler, B. (1990). "A marker at last for the devout hero of "Chariots of fire." *New York Times.* 12/02/1990.

Chapter 7

Sapolsky, R. (2004). Why zebras don't get ulcers: The acclaimed guide to stress, stress-related diseases, and coping. Third edition. New York: Henry Holt and Company.

Chapter 8

Phillips, A. (2013). "This is your life." Book review. Joan Acocella. The New Yorker. 02/25/2013.

Trueblood, D. (1951). *The life we Prize.* New York: Harper and Brothers Publishers.

Viorst, J. (1986). *Necessary losses: The loves, illusions, dependencies, and impossible expectations that all of us have to give up in order to grow.* New York: Simon and Schuster.

Chapter 9

Edelman, R. (2022). Society for American Baseball Research. Recovered on 02/03/2022.

Theodore, J. (2002). *Baseball's natural: The story of Eddie Waitkus.* Carbondale, IL: Southern Illinois University Press.

Chapter 10

Cousins, N. (2022). recovered from www.quotetab.com/quote/by-norman-cousins-free-will-and-determinism on 01/19/ 2022.

Dravecky, D. (2020). Recovered from "Get inspired." www.kalemati.net on 01/18/2022. (2020). Recovered from www.azquotes.com author>56255 Dave_Dravecky on 01/19/2022.

Strumpfer, W. (2018). "Interview with Dave Dravecky." Society for Baseball Research.

Chapter 12

Gifford, F. (1997). The NFL' greatest games. Polygram Video.

Gregg, F. (1997). The NFL's greatest games. Polygram Videos.

Lilly, B. (1997). The NFL's greatest games. Polygram Videos.

Mercein, C. (1997). The NFL's greatest games. Polygram Videos.

Maranass, D. (1999). *When pride still mattered.* New York: Simon and Schuster.

Myers, D. (2004). *Psychology*, eighth edition. New York: Worth Publishers.

Perkins, D. (1997). The NFL's greatest games. Polygram Videos.

Renfro, M. (1997). The NFL's greatest games. Polygram Videos.

Robinson, D. (1997). The NFL's greatest games. Polygram Videos.

Chapter 13

Robson, K. (1998). *A great and glorious game.* Chapel Hill, NC: Algonquin Books.

Chapter 14

Leavy, J. (2010). *The last boy: Mickey Mantle and the end of America's childhood.* New York: HarperCollins Publishers.

Chapter 17

Payne, D. (2020). "The fix: Why Jake LaMotta threw his 1947 fight with Billy Fox." Retrieved from www.Gambling.com on 01/02/2022.

Merron, J. (2008). "Real life: Raging bull." 01/07/2008. Recovered from ESPN.com on 01/02/2022.

Chapter 18

Moyle, C. (2012). Billy Miske: The St. Paul thunderbolt. International Boxing Research Organization announcement. 02/23/2012. Retrieved 12/29/2021.

Chapter 19

Gallaraga, A., Joyce, J. and Paisner, D. (2011). Nobody's perfect: Two men, one call, and a game for baseball history. New York: Atlantic Monthly Press.

Selig, B. (2022). Recovered from www.a-zquotes.com/author/ 31996 - Bud Selig on 02/08/2022.

Chapter 20

Giamatti, A. (1998). *A great and glorious game*. Chapel Hill, NC: Algonquin Books.

International Boxing Hall of Fame website. IBOF.com. Retrieved 06/15/2013.

Field of Dreams. (1989). Universal City, CA: Universal Pictures

About the Author

Max Malikow is a sports enthusiast who is on the faculty of the Renee Crown Honors Program of Syracuse University and an Adjunct Professor of Philosophy at LeMoyne College. He earned a Master's degree from Gordon-Conwell Theological Seminary and doctorate from Boston University. His previous books include *Why Be Good? And Other Questions Concerning Moral Philosophy, Heroism as Virtue*, and *Why Can't You Be More Like Me? An Introduction to Moral Philosophy.*

Made in the USA
Middletown, DE
25 August 2023